3

Sue :)

Love.

Diane Elchedi

# The TREASURE of CHRISTMAS

## A 25 DAY CELEBRATION

# The Treasure of Christmas

## A 25 Day Celebration

*Tim Dowdy*

Seed Publishing Group, LLC
Timmonsville, South Carolina

*The Treasure of Christmas*

Copyright © 2017 by Tim Dowdy

Published by:
Seed Publishing Group
2570 Double C Farm Ln
Timmonsville, SC 29161
seed–publishing–group.com

Seed Publishing Group is committed to bringing great resources to both individual Christians and the local church (please visit them at www.seed-publishing-group.com). As part of that commitment, they are partners with The Pillar Network for church planting (www.thepillarnetwork.com). $1 from each sale of *The Treasure of Christmas* goes directly to church plants throughout North America. Thank you for purchasing *The Treasure of Christmas*, and thank you for investing in church planting!

To order additional copies of this resource visit www.seed–publishing–group.com.

Library of Congress Control Number: 2017958801

ISBN–13: 978-0-9985451-1-0

Printed in the United States of America

*This is dedicated to my wife and best friend, Christie, and to our son and daughter-in-law, Micah and Kelly, along with our grandsons, Wyatt and Jack.*

This 25 day devotional began as a video series to our church family several years ago. I am so grateful for Eric Jackson, Spencer Watson and Abby Akins who filmed, edited and reviewed the material for each day. I am deeply indebted to numerous commentators and pastors who have served as a constant help understanding the great truths revealed in God's Word about the person and work of Jesus. I am especially grateful to my parents who always made sure that the birth of Jesus was the centerpiece of our family Christmas celebrations.

I'd like to say a heartfelt thank you to Jana Caison and her outstanding art students at Eagle's Landing Christian Academy for the amazing artwork they contributed to make this book such a beautiful keepsake.

Heather Boozer
Kaylah Bruno
Eunjin Choi
Savannah Fallaw
Alyssa Gjertsen
Candace Hill
Weronika Hipp
Jade Holmes
Luke Jones
Alyssa Mitchell
Mallory Poorman
A.J. Robinson
Madison Shelnutt
Jordyn Street
Emily Stuber
Olivia Tinsley
Katie Wallace
Joseph White
Bowen Ye
Victoria Zember

# Contents

*The Treasure of Christmas*

# Foreword

Several years ago, I had the splendid idea of buying a live Christmas tree for our family. My idea. My tree. Big plans. Bigger splash. And Mark becomes everyone's hero.

I drove to the tree lot, purchased the most gorgeous tree I could find, and drove home with a big grin. When I lugged it to the front porch, Melanie was waiting. She raised an eyebrow.

My heart sank. It usually sinks when Melanie raises an eyebrow, because that means that she's about to tell me something that had never crossed my mind.

"Have you measured the tree?" she asked.

Ummm.

I quickly realized why such a beautiful tree was still on the lot just a few days before Christmas. It was massive. I'm not a tool guy, so I didn't have a way to shorten the tree or trim its branches. I called a friend and borrowed everything I needed, but it was almost midnight when I got back home with the saw and clippers. I labored until I was sweating, and it was a cold winter's night. I had to trim it evenly so it still looked like a Christmas tree but was small enough to fit through the door.

Once I finally dragged the tree across the threshold, I shaped it a little more to take care of some of the damage I'd just created. That's when Melanie spoke up again.

"Hey, babe?" she said. That greeting is like her arched eyebrow. I always know I've messed up again when she calls out to me that way.

"Yeah," I answered.

"You know where the lights are, don't you?" she asked.

"In the attic, somewhere?"

"Nope," she said. "Do you remember last year when I told you that you should take off all the lights and store them, and you just didn't want to do that? You wanted to throw the whole thing away and get new ones for this year, remember?"

My heart sank again.

"You're going to Wal-Mart now."

My decision of convenience the year before was costing me now. I don't particularly care for stringing Christmas lights, but unstringing them is even worse—especially because of the tangled web my OCD weaves to cover every hole on the tree with a light.

I sighed and grabbed the car keys. The local Wal-Mart was open 24 hours, but by the time I got home and finished my masterpiece of artistry, it was 2 a.m. There I was, scheduled to speak at a Fellowship of Christian Athletes event early the next morning, and yet my head didn't hit the pillow until the wee hours. Somehow, I had let the tyranny of the moment overwhelm God's real heartbeat for the Christmas season.

Every passing year, it seems that more and more people lose focus on the real reason for Christmas. Don't you feel the hustle and bustle like I do? We don't think about a baby wrapped in swaddling clothes and lying in a manger. We think of gaudy house decorations and ornate Christmas trees. We don't think of herald angels singing glory to God in the highest. We think of the highest-priced gifts we can afford. We don't think of a Savior born to save us. We think, instead, of a store that can offer us savings.

My pastor for the last 16 years, Tim Dowdy, has written this great devotional to help us take the 25 days of the Christmas season and refocus them on their original purpose. That purpose has a name.

Jesus Christ is the Lamb of God sent to take away the sin of the world, and the miracle of God come to Earth in human form in the tiny Jewish hamlet of Bethlehem is the greatest story ever told—one that cannot and will not ever go away—no matter what the world says.

Let Pastor Tim's thoughts remind you that Jesus Christ is our only hope for joy, peace, and salvation. Let your heart be God's Bethlehem again this Christmas.

—Mark Hall

*Madison Shelnutt • 12ᵗʰ Grade*

# Introduction

Logs in the fireplace, snow covered rooftops, perfectly decorated trees and brightly colored presents. These are what most Christians imagine when we think of a setting for the celebration of the birth of Jesus. But I want us to start this journey in what might seems like an odd place for a connection to Christmas—just off the coast of Bermuda with a guy named Teddy.

Teddy Tucker has explored hundreds of shipwrecks in hopes of finding lost treasures. He championed the odd technique of discovering wreckage while floating high above the water in a chair, lifted by a helium balloon and towed behind a boat. His most intriguing find occurred after spotting some old sea-covered cannons in the Bermuda shallows about ten miles from the harbor. Five years later, while diving on that site, he took a water hose down to blast away the sand on the oceans floor. After the debris settled he saw it — a gold cross laying facedown in the sand. When he turned it over he was awestruck by the green emeralds embedded in its face. It was roughly crafted, which revealed that it was probably made by natives, yet it was amazingly beautiful. It remains his most treasured discovery.

The cross, later named Tucker's Cross, made its way to a museum that Tucker and his wife ran for the Bermuda government. In 1975, 20 years after Tucker's rare find, Queen

Elizabeth II was scheduled to visit the museum. However, right before her arrival it was discovered that the cross had been stolen and replaced by a replica without anyone noticing.

What does Tucker's Cross have to do with Christmas? On the surface, not much; yet a the story may be in the process of being repeated. With slow but steady progress, the celebration of the birth of Jesus is being stolen by a world that is letting the single most valuable expression of God's love slip right through its fingers.

To be honest, the theft of Christmas has been going on for such a long time, and so gradually, that most people - even Christians - see it but are not shaken by it. The worldly values and hardened hearts of people of the world come as no surprise to us. So, we blink and roll our eyes when a manger scene is banned from being displayed. We take a deep breath when the complaint, "Don't force your religious beliefs on me!", turns out the lights on a Jesus sign hanging in a store.

Sadly, if we continue down this path, one day people will gather to look at the treasures of Christmas without knowing the reason for this celebration. A replica will stand in place of the treasure, but this time it will look nothing like the original and will offer no hope, love, or joy to a world which is desperately in need of all three.

This is the reason I sat down to write twenty-five days of devotional thoughts about Christmas. God's love is more amazing and more valuable than anything else we treasure in this life. I want us to take each day of December to direct our hearts back to the "reason for the season." I hope to awaken our hearts to the most powerful way God's love has been displayed through Jesus. The Apostle John put it this way: "In this the love of God was made manifest among us, that God sent his only Son into the world, so that we might live through him (1 Jn 4:9).

Oh, and along the way, I hope to help rescue us from falling prey to the greatest theft in the history of the world. It should come as no surprise that the focus of each devotion is the person of Jesus.

The words of Jesus to a couple of discouraged disciples after his resurrection set the road map in place for each day. In the Gospel of Luke, Jesus appeared to two men leaving Jerusalem. His words to them serve as the model for our own walk towards Christmas Day.

*That very day two of them were going to a village named Emmaus, about seven miles from Jerusalem, and they were talking with each other about all these things that had happened. While they were talking and discussing together, Jesus himself drew near and went with them. But their eyes were kept from recognizing him. And he said to them, "What is this conversation that you are holding with each other as you walk?" And they stood still, looking sad. Then one of them, named Cleopas, answered him, "Are you the only visitor to Jerusalem who does not know the things that have happened there in these days?" And he said to them, "What things?" And they said to him, "Concerning Jesus of Nazareth, a man who was a prophet mighty in deed and word before God and all the people, and how our chief priests and rulers delivered him up to be condemned to death, and crucified him. But we had hoped that he was the one to redeem Israel. Yes, and besides all this, it is now the third day since these things happened. Moreover, some women of our company amazed us. They were at the tomb early in the morning, and when they did not find his body, they came back saying that they had even seen a vision of angels, who said that he was alive. Some of those who were with us went to the tomb and found it just as the women had said, but him they did not see." And he said to them, "O foolish ones, and slow of heart to believe all that the prophets have spoken! Was it not necessary that the Christ should suffer these things and enter into his glory?" **And beginning with***

3

> ***Moses and all the Prophets, he interpreted to them in all the Scriptures the things concerning himself*** *(Lk 24:13-27, emphasis mine).*

So, let's begin a simple walk through the Bible to take a look at *"all the Scriptures"* to be reminded of *"the things concerning"* Jesus until Christmas day, when we celebrate the birth of Jesus together. Whether December 25th finds you warming yourself by the fire on a cold winter day or on an island warmed by the sun, may you and your family worship and celebrate the true treasure of Christmas—his name is Jesus!

*Katie Wallace • 10ᵗʰ Grade*

# December 1

Today we start at the beginning - Genesis 1 - which is the first picture we see of Jesus in the Bible. God exists in the form of the Trinity, a word which describes Him in all His glory. I know that the word Trinity doesn't appear in the Bible, but it does accurately describe God the Father, God the Son, and God the Holy Spirit. These three are coequal, coeternal, and one God.

In the opening lines of Genesis, we see the announcement of the creation of the heavens and the earth, including the creation of light out of darkness.

> *In the beginning, God created the heavens and the earth. The earth was without form and void, and darkness was over the face of the deep. And the Spirit of God was hovering over the face of the waters. And God said, "Let there be light," and there was light. And God saw that the light was good. And God separated the light from the darkness. God called the light Day, and the darkness he called Night. And there was evening and there was morning, the first day (Gen 1:1–5).*

As we turn the pages of the Bible to the New Testament, we see that Jesus was present and involved in the creation. John writes:

> *In the beginning was the Word, and the Word was with God, and the Word was God. He was in the beginning with God. All things were made through him, and without him was not any thing made that was made. In him was life, and the life was the light of men (Jn 1:1-4).*

In verse 1, "Word" is capitalized, referring to a person; that person is Jesus. In the Creation account in Genesis 1:3, the Bible tells us that God the "Word" said, "Let there be light." The scripture ties this together beautifully from Genesis 1 to John 1, and even to 2 Corinthians, where the Apostle Paul made it even clearer:

> *For God, who said, "Let light shine out of darkness," has shone in our hearts to give the light of the knowledge of the glory of God in the face of Jesus Christ (2 Cor 4:6).*

"Let light shine out of darkness," is a direct quote from Genesis 1. In the beginning of the biblical record we see Jesus in Genesis 1 creating light, and then in John 1, Jesus *is* the light. There is physical light that allows us to see the beauty of God's creation. But the light the Bible speaks of here isn't a physical light. Jesus said of himself,

> *'I am the light of the world. Whoever follows me will not walk in darkness, but will have the light of life (Jn 8:12).'*

The spiritual light that Jesus spoke of is necessary for spiritual life. It is through Jesus that we see the truth concerning our sin and the truth concerning God's forgiveness. Jesus is the one who rescues us from the darkness and gives us life in his name. In fact, Jesus tells us that once a person follows him he or she will never again walk in darkness. To "follow" means to believe in Jesus for salvation; the result of trusting in Jesus is life and light.

Once we believe in Jesus, we come into the light, and we are to share the light. In Matthew 5:14-15, Christians are called the "light of the world" as well. We are to reflect the light of Jesus so that others can see him in us and experience the same joy of knowing Jesus, the true Light of the world!

that all peoples, nations, & languages SHOULD SERVE him

*Mallory Poorman • 10th Grade*

# December 2

Today, we're back in the book of Genesis again; this time in Genesis three. You may already know a little bit about this passage, because it records the Fall of Adam and Eve to sin. What we need to understand in this story, however, is that we see God punishing sin and providing a promise for restoration. What is evident in this chapter is that God's wrath against sin is overwhelmed by His mercy.

There is hope and help in the middle of God's judgment on sin. In fact, in Genesis 3:15, we see the very first pictures of the Gospel in the Bible. Remember, Gospel means "Good News," and there is hope even in judgment against sin.

*I will put enmity between you and the woman, and between your offspring and her offspring; he shall bruise your head, and you shall bruise his heel.*

What God is revealing to us in this text is that an offspring (descendant) of the woman would have his heel bruised by the serpent (Satan), but would himself crush the serpent's head. The offspring this passage speaks of is none other than Jesus.

The baby born in a manger came on a mission that was revealed to us in the opening book of the Bible. In other parts of the Bible the connection is made clearer.

> *The God of peace will soon crush Satan under your feet. The grace of our Lord Jesus Christ be with you (Rom 16:20).*
> *Since therefore the children share in flesh and blood, he himself likewise partook of the same things, that through death he might destroy the one who has the power of death, that is, the devil (Heb 2:14).*

In Genesis, we see the harsh realities of sin beginning to unfold—the serpent would crawl on his belly and be at odds with mankind; woman and man would feel sins effects in painful ways as well. Ultimately, death would be the greatest pain of sin.

The promise of hope is that sin would not reign forever. It would have a definite end, and there would be victory over sin in the person of Jesus. That victory would not be without a cost; we see that in the words, "You shall bruise his heel." While the language is metaphorical, the cost was real and the price great through the shedding of Christ Jesus' blood on the cross.

However, the death, burial, and resurrection of this same Jesus provided a crushing and complete blow to Satan and his workers of evil. Though Satan's final defeat and destiny is not made clear until the final book of the Bible, we know from the very first book that the victory is won through Jesus.

Genesis 3 gets us started down the path of understanding the "Good News" of the Gospel that is offered through Jesus. In the New Testament, we see Jesus sharing that same Gospel with a man named Nicodemus.

> *For God so loved the world, that he gave his only Son, that whoever believes in him should not perish but have eternal life.*

*For God did not send his Son into the world to condemn the world, but in order that the world might be saved through him (Jn 3:1–17).*

That Good News of Jesus is the reason we celebrate Christmas!

*A.J. Robinson • 7ʰ Grade*

# December 3

There is no doubt that Christmas as the celebration of the birth of Jesus is slowly being shifted off center stage by the world. The true meaning of Christmas has been lost in a flurry of other activities surrounding Christmastime gatherings. We must remember, however, that *Jesus* is still the reason that Christmas is a celebration at all. The birth of Jesus changed the world forever and, as a result, is the centerpiece of this day.

In the Old Testament, there are some very clear pictures foreshadowing the coming of the Savior. One of those is found in Genesis 22 in the exchange that took place between Abraham and Isaac. Isaac was Abraham's the long-awaited son. God had promised to give Abraham a son early in his life, but he had to wait until the later years of his life before his promised son was born. In fact, they named him Isaac, which means "laughter," because it was such good news of great joy.

Isaac brought such joy to this senior adult couple that the scene depicted in Genesis 22 seems unfathomable. The same God who promised the birth of Isaac, who delivered on that promise when it seemed impossible, came unexpectedly to Abraham and told him to sacrifice his one and only son. The conversation began this way:

> *After these things God tested Abraham and said to him, 'Abraham!' And he said, 'Here I am.' He said, 'Take your son, your only son Isaac, whom you love, and go to the land of Moriah, and offer him there as a burnt offering on one of the mountains of which I shall tell you (Gen 22:1–2).'*

And amazingly enough, Abraham obeyed God without question. Let's keep watching as Abraham and Isaac were headed to the place where the offering was to be made:

> *And Abraham took the wood of the burnt offering and laid it on Isaac his son. And he took in his hand the fire and the knife. So they went both of them together. And Isaac said to his father Abraham, 'My father!' And he said, 'Here I am, my son.' He said, 'Behold, the fire and the wood, but where is the lamb for a burnt offering?.' Abraham said, 'God will provide for himself the lamb for a burnt offering, my son.' So they went both of them together (Gen 22:6-8).*

From where we sit in history, we cannot help but think of another Son miraculously born and sacrificed. It reminds us of Jesus, born according to the promise of God. It also reminds us that God sacrificed *His* one and only Son, thereby providing the perfect sacrificial Lamb. What a beautiful picture of Jesus coming to be the offering for sin! In fact, John the Baptist said, "Behold, the Lamb of God, who takes away the sin of the world! (Jn 1:29)."

William Chatterton Dix was the manager of an insurance company when his life was devastated by a severe illness. He experienced personal revival in his life while recovering from the illness. This led him to compose several hymns expressing his faith. In 1865, he composed a hymn entitled "What Child is This?"

(one of my favorite Christmas carols), which speaks of the birth and death of Jesus, God's only begotten son. Notice the words,

*What Child is this who, laid to rest*
*On Mary's lap is sleeping?*
*Whom Angels greet with anthems sweet,*
*While shepherds watch are keeping?*

*This, this is Christ the King,*
*Whom shepherds guard and Angels sing;*
*Haste, haste, to bring Him laud,*
*The Babe, the Son of Mary.*

*Why lies He in such mean estate,*
*Where ox and ass are feeding?*
*Good Christians, fear, for sinners here*
*The silent Word is pleading.*

*Nails, spear shall pierce Him through,*
*The cross be borne for me, for you.*
*Hail, hail the Word made flesh,*
*The Babe, the Son of Mary.*

*So bring Him incense, gold and myrrh,*
*Come peasant, king to own Him;*
*The King of kings salvation brings,*
*Let loving hearts enthrone Him.*

*Raise, raise a song on high,*
*The virgin sings her lullaby.*
*Joy, joy for Christ is born,*
*The Babe, the Son of Mary.*

*The Treasure of Christmas*

I want to challenge you today to go back and read Genesis 22 - the story of Abraham and Isaac. It's a moving, powerful story! And as you read, remember the foreshadowing of the birth and death of Jesus, who is our hope for eternal life.

*Bowen Ye • 12<sup>th</sup> Grade*

# December 4

*A*s we continue our Christmas journey, I want us to travel back into the Old Testament again as we learn more about the birth of the Savior. This will help us discover that the entire Bible points us to Jesus. This time we make our way to the book of Joshua. Do you remember the story in chapter 5, when Joshua and the people of Israel were camped near the city of Jericho?

Joshua had been appointed by God to take the reins of leadership from Moses in order to guide Israel into the promised land. It was a daunting task to take over this role, but Joshua found courage in the promises of God and obeyed the call of God. After God miraculously provided a way for the Israelites to cross the Jordan River at flood stage, Joshua faced opposition in the Promised Land with courage and determination. Jericho was a fortified city that stood in the way of their conquest.

One night as Joshua visited the fortified walls of Jericho to determine what he needed to do to lead his army to victory over the city, he encountered a man standing before him with a sword drawn in his hand.

*And Joshua went to him and said to him, "Are you for us, or for our adversaries?" And he said, "No; but I am the com-*

> *mander of the army of the Lord. Now I have come." And Joshua fell on his face to the earth and worshiped and said to him, "What does my lord say to his servant?" And the commander of the Lord's army said to Joshua, "Take off your sandals from your feet, for the place where you are standing is holy." And Joshua did so (Josh 5:13-15).*

That last line reminds us of the encounter Moses had with God years before at the burning bush. That was the day Moses encountered God and was called to be the instrument he would use to lead the children of Israel out of Egyptian bondage. Now it was Joshua's turn.

There is some debate as to whether the man who stood before Joshua was the pre-incarnate Christ (an appearance of Christ before his birth) or an angel representing the Lord himself. One thing is certain: the Lord was making sure that Joshua knew who was in charge and that this battle would be won by God alone.

Joshua's second question was probably meant to give opportunity for the military strategy to be unveiled. Instead, Joshua was told to remove his unclean shoes because he was standing on holy ground.

This exchange outside the walls of the city of Jericho reminds us of something the Lord promised Joshua when he told him that he would become Moses's successor.

> *Have I not commanded you? Be strong and courageous. Do not be frightened, and do not be dismayed, for the Lord your God is with you wherever you go (Josh 1:9).*

The Lord told Joshua that the secret to his success as the leader of the Israelites was inseparably linked to God's divine presence—God would be with him. Hopefully, you remember the miraculous victory that God gave to Joshua and the Israelites at Jericho. God clearly demonstrated that he was with them.

When I think about the story of Joshua, I can't help but think about the birth of Jesus and the special name he was given. The name was first introduced in the Old Testament to refer to the future Messiah. Matthew quoted the prophet Isaiah in the first chapter of his gospel when he wrote,

> *Behold, the virgin shall conceive and bear a son, and they shall call his name Immanuel"* *(which means, God with us) (Matt 1:23).*

Yes! The Lord God is with us . . . and his name is Jesus!

*Luke Jones • 12ᵗʰ Grade*

# December 5

We're only 20 days away from the blessed day when we celebrate the birth of our Savior.

As we move toward Christmas, we must always remember that nothing could or should replace the centerpiece of this celebration—the birth of Jesus. You may be wondering why His birth so significant? The answer is powerful! Jesus is God in the flesh. He brings lasting hope through the good news of salvation in his name to every generation. That message is consistently proclaimed in the Old Testament and in the New Testament.

*The Spirit of the Lord God is upon me,*
*because the Lord has anointed me*
*to bring good news to the poor;*
*he has sent me to bind up the brokenhearted,*
*to proclaim liberty to the captives,*
*and the opening of the prison to those who are bound;*
*to proclaim the year of the Lord's favor,*
*and the day of vengeance of our God;*
*to comfort all who mourn (Is 61:1-2).*

This passage in the Old Testament was written hundreds of years before Jesus came to this earth in the flesh. Then, in

Luke 4, we see an episode in the life of Jesus that ties the message proclaimed in Isaiah 61 with Jesus himself.

In Jesus' day, a synagogue service normally consisted of prayers, oral readings of the law and prophets, and a sermon. The leader of the service would stand to read and pray, but he would sit to teach the message. That Jesus was asked to participate in the reading was not an odd request, since others were often invited to participate in the service. It was also no accident that Jesus was given the scroll of Isaiah the prophet to read. Here is the account:

> *And he came to Nazareth, where he had been brought up. And as was his custom, he went to the synagogue on the Sabbath day, and he stood up to read.*
> *And the scroll of the prophet Isaiah was given to him. He unrolled the scroll and found the place where it was written,*
> *The Spirit of the Lord is upon me,*
> *because he has anointed me*
> *to proclaim good news to the poor.*
> *He has sent me to proclaim liberty to the captives*
> *and recovering of sight to the blind,*
> *to set at liberty those who are oppressed,*
> *to proclaim the year of the Lord's favor.'*
> *And he rolled up the scroll and gave it back to the attendant and sat down. And the eyes of all in the synagogue were fixed on him (Lk 4:16-22).*

Notice, Jesus read Isaiah 61:1-2 and shared a message with those listening. And as the people gathered listened to Jesus read, they were amazed. This section of Luke probably records only one of the statements Jesus shared with them, but it was remarkably powerful. Jesus looked at them and said,

*'Today this Scripture has been fulfilled in your hearing.' And all spoke well of him and marveled at the gracious words that were coming from his mouth (Lk 4:21-22).*

Jesus declared that the prophecy had a present fulfillment, and He was the one upon whom the Spirit dwelt. The hope and salvation the people longed for was sitting before them in human form—Jesus of Nazareth. God's only son had arrived, the one who had been foretold in the scriptures hundreds of years before.

Jesus is the long-awaited Messiah; the Savior of the world.

*Jordyn Street • 11<sup>th</sup> Grade*

# December 6

As we make our way to the celebration of Christmas, we are looking at some different pictures of Jesus in the scriptures. For the next three days, I want to look at some of the descriptive images of Jesus. Today, we're going to consider Jesus as the Son of Man.

The Old Testament holds some valuable insights regarding the expression, the "Son of Man."

> I saw in the night visions,
> and behold, with the clouds of heaven
>    there came one like a son of man,
> and he came to the Ancient of Days
>    and was presented before him.
> And to him was given dominion
>    and glory and a kingdom,
> that all peoples, nations, and languages
>    should serve him;
> his dominion is an everlasting dominion,
>    which shall not pass away,
> and his kingdom one
>    that shall not be destroyed (Dan 7:13-14).

That phrase, "Son of Man," may not sound very import-ant until we read the same words in the New Testament. Jesus used those very same words to describe Himself. In fact, it's the phrase he used the most when describing himself. You might re-member the time when Jesus entered Jericho and encountered a tax collector named Zaccheus. This man had selfishly defrauded people through the deeds of his wicked heart. But when he met Jesus, his life was changed. After spending time with Zaccheus and working in his life, Jesus said to him,

> *Today salvation has come to this house, since he also is a son of Abraham. For the Son of Man came to seek and to save the lost (Lk 19:9-10).*

This expression—Son of Man—helps us understand that Jesus was fully human in every way. Jesus was born in Bethlehem as a human being; therefore, he was letting everyone know that he could identify with the human race, because he took on flesh. That same phrase also connected with the prophecy in the book of Daniel which revealed that the Son of Man was a heavenly figure. That the Son of Man would come "with the clouds of heaven" reminds us that this person would be more than just a man (Dan 7:13).

At other times Jesus used "Son of God" to reveal that he was fully human *and* fully God. These two descriptions describe the uniqueness of Jesus—he is the only begotten son of God. It is his birth that we celebrate at Christmas!

I want to close today's devotion with these words from the Apostle Paul to the church in Philippi:

> *Have this mind among yourselves, which is yours in Christ Jesus, who, though he was in the form of God, did not count*

*equality with God a thing to be grasped, but emptied himself, by taking the form of a servant, being born in the likeness of men. And being found in human form, he humbled himself by becoming obedient to the point of death, even death on a cross. Therefore God has highly exalted him and bestowed on him the name that is above every name, so that at the name of Jesus every knee should bow, in heaven and on earth and under the earth, and every tongue confess that Jesus Christ is Lord, to the glory of God the Father (Phil 2:5–11).*

*Emily Stuber* •11*th* *Grade*

# December 7

As we continue to examine pictures of Jesus in the scriptures, today we add the image of Jesus as "Priest" and "King."

Understanding Jesus as our "Priest" comes through a rather mysterious character in the Bible named Melchizedek.

> *The Lord has sworn*
> *and will not change his mind,*
> *"You are a priest forever*
> *after the order of Melchizedek (Ps 110:4).*

Melchizedek was not only king of Salem; he was also a priest of the Most High God. The term "Salem" means peace, so Melchizedek was literally the "King of Peace." We also see this term being used in the book of Hebrews with one differende— Jesus is our High Priest.

> *Therefore he had to be made like his brothers in every respect,*
> *so that he might become a merciful and faithful high priest in*
> *the service of God, to make propitiation for the sins of the*
> *people (Heb 2:17).*

> *Since then we have a great high priest who has passed through the heavens, Jesus, the Son of God, let us hold fast our confession (Heb 4:14).*

In biblical times, the priest was the mediator between the people of God and God Himself. He offered sacrifices on behalf of the people. Also, the role was reserved for one who was holy and set apart to serve the living God. Jesus shared this title because he came for this very purpose. He was not like other priests, however. Jesus was ordained to be our High Priest. He wasn't chosen from among men as others before him. Instead, he *became* a man to serve as our high priest. Jesus didn't continually need to offer sacrifices; rather, he offered himself as the sacrifice for sins – once for all – for those who trust in God through him. He didn't offer the blood of animals; rather, he offered his own blood as the full payment for the sins of humanity. The writer of Hebrews put it this way:

> *He entered once for all into the holy places, not by means of the blood of goats and calves but by means of his own blood, thus securing an eternal redemption (Heb 9:12).*

Jesus is also King! At his birth, the Bible records that the Magi came inquiring of King Herod where they could find the King of the Jews. Matthew wrote:

> *Now after Jesus was born in Bethlehem of Judea in the days of Herod the king, behold, wise men from the east came to Jerusalem, saying, "Where is he who has been born king of the Jews? For we saw his star when it rose and have come to worship him." When Herod the king heard this, he was troubled, and all Jerusalem with him; and assembling all the chief*

*priests and scribes of the people, he inquired of them where the Christ was to be born. They told him, "In Bethlehem of Judea, for so it is written by the prophet: 'And you, O Bethlehem, in the land of Judah, are by no means least among the rulers of Judah; for from you shall come a ruler who will shepherd my people Israel.'" Then Herod summoned the wise men secretly and ascertained from them what time the star had appeared. And he sent them to Bethlehem, saying, "Go and search diligently for the child, and when you have found him, bring me word, that I too may come and worship him." After listening to the king, they went on their way. And behold, the star that they had seen when it rose went before them until it came to rest over the place where the child was. When they saw the star, they rejoiced exceedingly with great joy. And going into the house, they saw the child with Mary his mother, and they fell down and worshiped him. Then, opening their treasures, they offered him gifts, gold and frankincense and myrrh (Matt 2:1–11).*

We see the depiction of Jesus as King in other areas of scripture as well. At the end of his Jesus' life, Pontius Pilate asked him, "Are you the King of the Jews (Lk 23:3)?" Jesus confirmed that he was . . . and that led to his crucifixion. Finally, in the book of Revelation, the Apostle John applied the expression, "King of kings and Lord of lords," to Jesus, meaning that there was no higher authority in heaven or earth. Jesus is the King.

Jesus fulfilled both of these roles. He is the King of kings and the Lord of lords. And, he is also the Great High Priest of the saints. He is the One who holds our lives in his hands as the King of the ages. He is also the One that holds on to us, because He himself is our sacrifice; he is our Mediator; he is our Savior; he is our Great High Priest and King!

*Victoria Zember • 9ᵗʰ Grade*

# December 8

Today, we're looking at the third picture of Jesus in the Bible—Jesus as "Prophet." As we look in the Old Testament, we see glimpses of this term being used to describe Jesus.

> *I will raise up for them a prophet like you from among their brothers. And I will put my words in his mouth, and he shall speak to them all that I command him (Deut 18:18).*

Throughout God's work in the lives of people, prophets fulfilled an important role in the history of Israel; they brought the word of God to the people of Israel.

Sometimes even unbelieving nations like Nineveh needed to be exposed to the word of God and to hear the word of God. So, God would raise up someone like Jonah to take God's prophetic message to them.

Jesus came as a Prophet of God as well, proclaiming the truth of the Kingdom of God. In fact, in one of his very first messages he proclaimed, "Repent, for the kingdom of Heaven is at hand (Mt 3:2)." While his message was difficult for some to hear, Jesus made it clear that he had authority from heaven to speak with power, because he spoke only what He heard from God the Father.

> *So Jesus answered them, 'My teaching is not mine, but his who sent me (Jn 7:16).'*

> *'I have much to say about you and much to judge, but he who sent me is true, and I declare to the world what I have heard from him (Jn 8:26).'*

> *So Jesus said to them, 'When you have lifted up the Son of Man, then you will know that I am he, and that I do nothing on my own authority, but speak just as the Father taught me (Jn 8:28).'*

> *For I have not spoken on my own authority, but the Father who sent me has himself given me a commandment—what to say and what to speak (Jn 12:49).*

Jesus acted as the prophet of God declaring truth from God. He also acted as a prophet as he delivered the message of God to the world concerning the future. Prophets in the Old Testament often were given messages that applied to the events of the future; Jesus delivered the message of God concerning the future of all things as well. Similarly, Jesus served as a prophet of God when he performed miracles. When John the Baptist was in prison, certain of his own death, he sent men to Jesus to ask about his identity. Jesus responded by referring to his miracles.

> *And when the men had come to him, they said, 'John the Baptist has sent us to you, saying, 'Are you the one who is to come, or shall we look for another?' In that hour he healed many people of diseases and plagues and evil spirits, and on many who were blind he bestowed sight. And he answered them, 'Go and tell John what you have seen and heard: the blind receive*

*their sight, the lame walk, lepers are cleansed, and the deaf hear, the dead are raised up, the poor have good news preached to them. And blessed is the one who is not offended by me (Lk 7:20-23).'*

In the Old Testament book of Deuteronomy, God told Moses that in the future He would send another prophet to Israel: "And I will put my words in his mouth. He will tell them everything I command him (Deut 18:18)." The prophet that God spoke about was Jesus. In fact, one remarkable reason we celebrate Jesus' birth is that He is *the* Prophet, because he is the living Word of God to the world. John explained it this way:

> *In the beginning was the Word, and the Word was with God, and the Word was God. He was in the beginning with God. All things were made through him, and without him was not any thing made that was made…And the Word became flesh and dwelt among us, and we have seen his glory, glory as of the only Son from the Father, full of grace and truth (Jn 1:1-3, 14).*

*Candace Hill • 12<sup>th</sup> Grade*

# December 9

I am a bit old fashioned when it comes to the celebration of Christmas—I love singing traditional Christian hymns. One of my favorite hymns was written by Charles Wesley entitled, "Hark! The Herald Angels Sing," which was introduced through a hymn collection in 1739, but revised twice. In 1754 Charles Wesley's friend and fellow Christian leader, George Whitefield, made a dramatic change to the first line and a few other changes as well. Then in 1961, the version that we sing today was published in another collection of Christmas hymns. I can almost hear the music playing as the celebration begins…

> *Hark! the herald angels sing,*
> *"Glory to the newborn King.*
> *Peace on earth and mercy mild*
> *God and sinners reconciled!"*
> *Joyful, all ye nations, rise;*
> *Join the triumph of the skies;*
> *With the angelic hosts proclaim,*
> *"Christ is born in Bethlehem!"*
> *Hark, the herald angels sing,*
> *"Glory to the newborn King!"*

This hymn stands among a trio of popular hymns which were written to celebrate the angels announcement of the birth of Jesus to the shepherds on that glorious night. The other two, "O Little Town of Bethlehem" and "Silent Night," join Wesley's hymn in proclaiming that Jesus is "Christ the Lord."

This one revelation made Jesus' birth remarkable and worthy of an angelic proclamation. The angels announcement to the shepherds has always been one of my favorite parts of the Christmas story to read on Christmas Eve. Luke, the physician, recorded the events surrounding the announcement this way:

> *And an angel of the Lord appeared to them, and the glory of the Lord shone around them, and they were filled with great fear. And the angel said to them, 'Fear not, for behold, I bring you good news of great joy that will be for all the people. For unto you is born this day in the city of David a Savior, who is Christ the Lord. And this will be a sign for you: you will find a baby wrapped in swaddling cloths and lying in a manger.' And suddenly there was with the angel a multitude of the heavenly host praising God and saying, 'Glory to God in the highest, and on earth peace among those with whom he is pleased!' When the angels went away from them into heaven, the shepherds said to one another, 'Let us go over to Bethlehem and see this thing that has happened, which the Lord has made known to us (Lk 2:9-15).'*

The awe-inspiring announcement revealed that this baby "is Christ the Lord." The word translated as "Christ" in English comes from the Greek word Χριστός (Christos). That word is a translation of the Hebrew word חישמ (Meshiakh) which means "anointed," and is often written in the Bible as "Messiah."

The announcement of the angels to the shepherds that night meant that the long-awaited Anointed One was finally here!

In the Gospel of John, the Apostle recorded this confession of Andrew,

> *One of the two who heard John speak and followed Jesus was Andrew, Simon Peter's brother. He first found his own brother Simon and said to him, "We have found the Messiah (which means Christ) (Jn 1:40-41).*

John made another statement regarding Jesus as Messiah:

> *Who is the liar but he who denies that Jesus is the Christ (1 Jn 2:22)?*

Jesus is the Christ, which means that he is the one who would suffer and die for the sins of the world. Yet, he would defeat sin and death through his resurrection. In Acts 2, the words of Peter revealed the importance of the resurrection of Jesus the Christ,

> *Brothers, I may say to you with confidence about the patriarch David that he both died and was buried, and his tomb is with us to this day. Being therefore a prophet, and knowing that God had sworn with an oath to him that he would set one of his descendants on his throne, he foresaw and spoke about the resurrection of the Christ, that he was not abandoned to Hades, nor did his flesh see corruption. This Jesus God raised up, and of that we all are witnesses (Acts 2:29-32).*

Jesus is the Christ, the Messiah; the one who suffered and died for sin; the one who was raised from the dead to live forever, and to make a way for us to live forever, too!

*Luke Jones • 12<sup>th</sup> Grade*

# December 10

I t's hard to that believe we're now 10 days into the month of December. Already, our minds and hearts are preparing us for the celebration of the birth of Jesus with our families and friends. Visions of turkey and dressing, Christmas cookies, and other family traditions stir our memories as we prepare to celebrate with our loved ones. And though this special time with family is precious to us, we must remember the real reason for the season—Jesus!

As we reflect on the pictures of Jesus in the Bible, it's helpful to connect the Old Testament prophecies concerning Jesus with the New Testament fulfillments of those prophecies. That's what I intend for us to do over the next few days.

Today, we will begin with the prophecy announced in Genesis 12:3—that Jesus would be a descendant from the line of Abraham.

> *Now the Lord said to Abram, "Go from your country and your kindred and your father's house to the land that I will show you. And I will make of you a great nation, and I will bless you and make your name great, so that you will be a bless-ing. I will bless those who bless you, and him who dishonors*

> *you I will curse, and in you all the families of the earth shall be blessed (Gen 12:1–3).*

That prophetic message was given by God to Abraham. Then, Matthew wrote this:

> *The book of the genealogy of Jesus Christ, the son of David, the son of Abraham (Mt 1:1).*

Matthew opened his gospel narrative by naming Jesus as the son of David and the son of Abraham, both of which revealed that Jesus was of Jewish descent in the royal line of the greatest king of the Israelites.

Let me read you what one commentator wrote about this:

> *The "Son of Abraham" traces Jesus' lineage back to the founding father of the nation of Israel, thus ensuring his Jewish pedigree from the earliest stage of his people's history. But echoes are probably also to be heard here of God's promises to Abraham that his offspring would bless all the peoples of the earth. "Son of Abraham" also carried messianic overtones as well in at least some intertestamental Jewish circles (Craig L. Blomberg, The New American Commentary: Matthew, vol. 22, Nashville: Broadman & Holman, 1992, 52).*

As we see the family connection of Jesus to David and Abraham, we also see the link to the promises God made to each of these men. It reminds us that God had a plan from the very beginning, and His plan was going to be fulfilled through the person of Jesus. In Jesus, all the promises made to Abraham are fulfilled. In Jesus, the rightful heir of the throne of David is found. But there is something else that is important to note—these men were instruments of God as he worked out his plan for the redemption of mankind. Their lives reveal the need for Jesus and the hope found only in him.

All of these men were sinners, just as we are all sinners. Their sin demonstrates their need for a Savior. We can read the story of their lives and see the evidence of sin—Abraham, among other things, was a liar; David a murder and adulterer. If we were to look over the lists provided in the genealogies in Matthew and Luke, we would see sinner after sinner. All were sinners in need of a savior, and that Savior is Jesus.

> *For our sake he made him to be sin who knew no sin, so that in him we might become the righteousness of God (2 Cor 5:21).*

Philips Brooks (1868) said it best through the words of a now well-known Christmas carol:

> *O little town of Bethlehem,*
> *How still we see thee lie.*
> *Above thy deep and dreamless sleep*
> *The silent stars go by;*
> *Yet in thy dark streets shineth*
> *The everlasting Light;*
> *The hopes and fears of all the years*
> *Are met in thee tonight.*

*Olivia Tinsley • 10<sup>th</sup> Grade*

# December 11

*L*et's continue to look at the prophecies about Jesus in the Old Testament which are fulfilled in the New Testament. Prophecy in the Bible is much more about telling the truth about the present than it is about predicting the future. There are times in the biblical record that we see prophecies concerning the future, however; especially concerning the arrival of Jesus.

Today, we look at a very unique picture in the Old Testament, which prophecies that Jesus will be born of a virgin. Now of course, this is impossible—apart from a miraculous work of God, that is.

> *Therefore the Lord himself will give you a sign. Behold, the virgin shall conceive and bear a son, and shall call his name Immanuel (Is 7:14).*

This prophecy, proclaimed several hundred years before Jesus was born, may seem rather foolish. How could a virgin possibly bear a child? But when we turn to the New Testament, we see the fulfillment of that prophecy in precise detail.

> *Now the birth of Jesus Christ took place in this way. When his mother Mary had been betrothed to Joseph, before they came*

*together she was found to be with child from the Holy Spirit. And her husband Joseph, being a just man and unwilling to put her to shame, resolved to divorce her quietly. But as he considered these things, behold, an angel of the Lord appeared to him in a dream, saying, "Joseph, son of David, do not fear to take Mary as your wife, for that which is conceived in her is from the Holy Spirit. She will bear a son, and you shall call his name Jesus, for he will save his people from their sins." All this took place to fulfill what the Lord had spoken by the prophet: "Behold, the virgin shall conceive and bear a son, and they shall call his name Immanuel" (which means, God with us). When Joseph woke from sleep, he did as the angel of the Lord commanded him: he took his wife, but knew her not until she had given birth to a son. And he called his name Jesus (Matt 1:18-25).*

What an amazing prophecy—seemingly impossible, but incredibly accurate!

There are some who look for ways to discredit Christianity and the divinity of Jesus. They claim that the story of the virgin birth may have originated from the myths and legends of pagan religions. Still other critics of Christianity use the virgin birth as a way to ridicule our faith and mock this doctrine as mystical or anti-intellectual. One retired Episcopal bishop argued that the idea of the virgin birth was just an exaggeration invented by early Christians to emphasize the divine nature of Jesus.

So, if there are doubters and critics of the virgin birth, then there is one question that must be answered: Why is it so important to believe this biblical truth about the birth of Jesus?

There is a clear, simple answer to that question—the virgin birth is clearly taught in the Gospels, so to deny the virgin birth is to deny the authority of the Bible. But a greater reason comes from asking another question: If Jesus was not conceived of the Holy Spirit then who was his father? There is no human answer that could explain the virgin birth—except the truth itself.

The virgin birth explains how Jesus can be both fully God and fully man. The virgin birth reveals how Jesus could be born without a sin nature and be qualified to die for our sins as the perfect, substitute sacrifice—"the Lamb of God (Jn 1:29)." The virgin birth displays the amazing compassion and grace of God to offer salvation and hope to the world.

> *For God so loved the world, that he gave his only Son, that whoever believes in him should not perish but have eternal life (Jn 3:16).*

*Alyssa Gjertsen • 11th Grade*

# December 12

The past few days we have been looking at Messianic prophecies in the Old Testament which are fulfilled in the New Testament through the birth of Jesus. Today, we focus another prophecy concerning the family line into which Jesus would be born. We have already discussed how Jesus was a descendant of Abraham; today we add the names of Isaac and of Jacob.

The first dot in this prophetic line begins in Genesis. God told Abraham that he would bless him by making his family line into a great nation. Further, because of Abraham, all the nations of the earth would be blessed (Gen 12:3). Abraham may have had his doubts about how this promise could be fulfilled, since he was already old and still childless. However, in Genesis 17, God restated his promise and changed his name from Abram to Abraham; then, he changed Abraham's wife's name from Sarai to Sarah. Still, Abraham cried out, "Oh, that Ishmael might live before you." Abraham thought that he was too old to have a child with Sarah. But God had other plans.

> God said, "No, but Sarah your wife shall bear you a son, and you shall call his name Isaac. I will establish my covenant with him as an everlasting covenant for his offspring after him (Gen 17:19).

53

Now let's jump ahead a bit in the Old Testament and read a phrase that will become a favorite expression to describe God.

> *God also said to Moses, "Say this to the people of Israel: 'The Lord, the God of your fathers, the God of Abraham, the God of Isaac, and the God of Jacob, has sent me to you.' This is my name forever, and thus I am to be remembered throughout all generations (Ex 3:15).*

When we examine the names mentioned in these passages, and then turn to the New Testament, we see prophecy fulfilled in the genealogy recorded in the opening chapter of Matthew.

> *Abraham was the father of Isaac, and Isaac the father of Jacob, and Jacob the father of Judah and his brothers…and Jacob the father of Joseph the husband of Mary, of whom Jesus was born, who is called Christ (Mt 1:2,16).*

If that isn't proof enough, we can turn to Acts 3 and read the proclamation that Apostle Peter made to the people following an amazing miracle.

> *Men of Israel, why do you wonder at this, or why do you stare at us, as though by our own power or piety we have made him walk? The God of Abraham, the God of Isaac, and the God of Jacob, the God of our fathers, glorified his servant Jesus, whom you delivered over and denied in the presence of Pilate, when he had decided to release him (Acts 3:12–13).*

Peter used the same combination of names that God had used when speaking with Moses in Exodus 3. This is more than just a formula; it is the legacy of a covenant-keeping God.

Scripture records that upon Abraham's death he left everything to his son Isaac. God told Isaac that he would keep his covenant to Abraham through him.

> *"Sojourn in this land, and I will be with you and will bless you, for to you and to your offspring I will give all these lands, and I will establish the oath that I swore to Abraham your father (Gen 26:3)."*

When Isaac was blessed with twin boys, the Lord made it clear that he would fulfill his promise through the younger son, Jacob.

Then the Lord appeared to Jacob in a dream and reiterated the same promise.

> *And behold, the Lord stood above it and said, "I am the Lord, the God of Abraham your father and the God of Isaac. The land on which you lie I will give to you and to your offspring. Your offspring shall be like the dust of the earth, and you shall spread abroad to the west and to the east and to the north and to the south, and in you and your offspring shall all the families of the earth be blessed (Gen 28:13–14)."*

This name of God significantly impacts our celebration of Christmas by reminding us that he is a covenant-keeping God. Jesus' birth was the fulfillment of his promise, and it is in Jesus that all the promises of God will be fulfilled. Just as Abraham, Isaac, and Jacob could look forward to the future because of the promises of God, we can look forward to the future too, knowing that the Lord will bring to pass all that he has promised to us!

*Joseph White • 9th Grade*

# December 13

J've really enjoyed taking each day to examine the pictures of Jesus found throughout the Bible. One of the things I hope you've noticed is that there is no shortage of prophecies in the Old Testament about the birth of Jesus. And the detail of these prophecies is mind-boggling. These prophecies remind us over and over again that from the very beginning God has always had a plan for our redemption, our hope, our life—and that plan was fulfilled in Jesus.

One of the prophecies about the birth of Jesus that is particularly interesting is recorded in the book of Micah. This short book of prophecy, written around 700 BC, identifies that exact place of the birth of Jesus—Amazing!

> *But you, O Bethlehem Ephrathah, who are too little to be among the clans of Judah, from you shall come forth for me one who is to be ruler in Israel, whose coming forth is from of old, from ancient days (Micah 5:2).*

The New Testament accounts in Matthew and Luke record the fulfillment of that prophecy.

> *And assembling all the chief priests and scribes of the people, he inquired of them where the Christ was to be born. They told him, 'In Bethlehem of Judea, for so it is written by the prophet: 'And you, O Bethlehem, in the land of Judah, are by no means least among the rulers of Judah; for from you shall come a ruler who will shepherd my people Israel (Matt 2:4–6).'*

We can infer from this account that Matthew intended to draw attention to the fact that the birth of Jesus was the fulfillment of prophecy.

Luke, on the other hand, was writing to the Gentiles, so his purpose was to reveal the humble circumstances surrounding the birth of the Savior of the world. Joseph and Mary began their journey in Nazareth, which would have been about a 60-mile journey to the town of Bethlehem. This would have been at least a three-day walk, since Nazareth was in the northern town of Galilee, and Bethlehem was about six miles south of Jerusalem. Even though they had to travel south, the scriptures say that they "went up from Galilee," because Bethlehem was in the hills (Lk 2:3). This would have been a difficult journey, especially for Mary, who was about eight months pregnant.

When the Joseph and Mary finally arrived in Bethlehem, the boarding houses were already full. There was no room for the weary couple. Traditions surrounding our Christmas celebrations have led us to believe that Jesus was born in a stable or cave, but we don't know that for sure. Luke's account of Jesus' birth states that Mary wrapped Jesus in strips of cloth and laid him in a manger, which was a feeding trough for animals (Lk 2:7). What we know for sure is that Jesus was born in a place where animals were kept. Even though we don't know the exact place in Bethlehem where Jesus was born, we do know that his birth fulfilled

Old Testament prophecies. This was a humble beginning for the "Anointed One."

A humble beginning in an insignificant town; yet it is the most significant thing to ever happen on this planet. Jesus was born in the town of Bethlehem to be the Savior of the world. The Gospel really is the good news, and it has always been God's plan to provide salvation through Jesus.

*Olivia Tinsley • 10<sup>th</sup> Grade*

# December 14

J'm not sure anyone knows who first said that "A picture is worth a thousand words," but we all know it's the truth. Pictures can make us cry or bring us joy, spark our memories or remind us of yesterday. Pictures are powerful—even word pictures. Sometimes, pictures provide answers to questions or give evidence that yields a more complete understanding of an event.

Such is the case with what we will read from the prophet Hosea today. Prophecies like this one are pictures to help us see God's redemptive plan through the miraculous incarnation of Jesus.

We have very few details about the life of Hosea, but we know that his name means "salvation." Hosea lived at about the same time as two other prophets: Micah and Isaiah. He received a rather unique calling by God—he was commanded to marry a woman named Gomer and have children with her.

This command may not sound strange at first, until you actually read the opening lines of the book of Hosea. When you do, you'll discover a surprising fact about her—she was a prostitute. In fact, Hosea's prophecies came from his own personal life experiences. The unfaithfulness of his wife mirrored the unfaithfulness of Israel toward God. The naming of his children revealed God's judgment upon Israel. However, even in pronouncing judgment, this book contains a statement meant to remind Israel of the amazing way that God cared for them. It says simply,

> *"When Israel was a child, I loved him, and out of Egypt I called my son (Hosea 11:1)."*

In this passage we see that God called his son out of bondage in Egypt. He was acting as a kind and loving Father. When the nation of Israel was hopelessly trapped in slavery, God—full of compassion—gave them help and hope by delivering them from the oppressive rule of the Egyptians. However, though Israel enjoyed the deliverance provided by God the Father, they would struggle to listen or obey him. Their hard hearts were revealed time and again as they rebelled against their loving Father-God. Because of their disobedience, God poured out judgment upon his people. That discipline was always administered with a loving purpose : to redeem his children, Israel.

In his account of the life of Jesus, Matthew showed that this prophecy in Hosea had been fulfilled through the events following his birth in Bethlehem.

> *Now when they had departed, behold, an angel of the Lord appeared to Joseph in a dream and said, 'Rise, take the child and his mother, and flee to Egypt, and remain there until I tell you, for Herod is about to search for the child, to destroy him.' And he rose and took the child and his mother by night and departed to Egypt and remained there until the death of Herod. This was to fulfill what the Lord had spoken by the prophet, 'Out of Egypt I called my son (Matt 2:13-15).'*

One of the things I love about this passage is that Matthew wrote, "This was to fulfill what Lord had spoken of by the prophet." There is some confusion surrounding this passage, and many scholars have studied and written about why Matthew penned those particular words. In Matthew's heart there was no confusion, however; the trip to Egypt fulfilled this prophecy concerning Jesus.

I'm not going to pretend to have all of the answers to the questions concerning Matthew's use of this prophecy. But one thing is clear—God's deliverance of Israel from slavery in Egypt directly mirrored the return of Jesus to Israel from Egypt after Herod's death.

What do we learn from today's passages of scripture? We see very clearly that God always had a plan for our redemption—that plan was always to send Jesus to be the Messiah of Israel and the Savior of the world. He is our Redeemer; our great God and King.

And that's why Christmas is the greatest time of the year!

*Alyssa Mitchell • 11ᵗʰ Grade*

# December 15

We are just 10 days from the celebration of the birth of Jesus on Christmas Day! Can't you feel the air buzzing with anticipation?

Let's continue our exciting journey through the pages of scripture. The pictures of Christ found in the Old Testament are numerous, and each of one of them helps us see the plan of God for our salvation through the person and work of Jesus.

Today, we look at another prophecy that foretold the miraculous coming of Jesus. This prophecy outlines the fact that a forerunner would come to prepare the way for the Messiah, Jesus. We find this prophecy in two places in the Old Testament.

*A voice cries: 'In the wilderness prepare the way of the Lord; make straight in the desert a highway for our God (Is 40:3).'*

*Behold, I send my messenger, and he will prepare the way before me. And the Lord whom you seek will suddenly come to his temple; and the messenger of the covenant in whom you delight, behold, he is coming, says the Lord of hosts (Mal 3:1).'*

In Isaiah, this forerunner is simply called "a voice," and in Malachi he is called "my messenger." When we turn to the

New Testament, it's easy to identify who these writings were about—John the Baptist. Mark, the writer of the gospel account that bears his name, left no doubt as to how we should interpret these prophecies. Though he only mentions the prophet Isaiah by name, both passages are included in his opening lines:

> *The beginning of the gospel of Jesus Christ, the Son of God. As it is written in Isaiah the prophet, 'Behold, I send my messenger before your face, who will prepare your way, the voice of one crying in the wilderness: 'Prepare the way of the Lord, make his paths straight,' John appeared, baptizing in the wilderness and proclaiming a baptism of repentance for the forgiveness of sins (Mk 1:1–4).*

Mark clearly identifies the people that Isaiah and Malachi spoke about—John is the "messenger," and Jesus is "the Lord." God's plan for salvation was being fulfilled!

John the Baptist was a fascinating figure. He was rough and rugged—we know that by the description of his wardrobe and his unique diet. His clothes were similar to those of the prophet Elijah.

> *Now John was clothed with camel's hair and wore a leather belt around his waist and ate locusts and wild honey (Mk 1:6).*

John the Baptist was a messenger from God with a clear and simple message: "Repent, for the kingdom of heaven is at hand (Matt 3:2)." His purpose was clear as well; he was to prepare the way for the Lord. John's popularity grew in spite of his straightforward, confrontational message, yet he knew that he was simply a servant of God fulfilling his call to make things ready for

Jesus. Even when people questioned him about his identity, John knew his place and purpose.

> *And this is the testimony of John, when the Jews sent priests and Levites from Jerusalem to ask him, 'Who are you?' He confessed, and did not deny, but confessed, 'I am not the Christ.' And they asked him, 'What then? Are you Elijah?' He said, 'I am not. 'Are you the Prophet?' And he answered, 'No.' So they said to him, 'Who are you? We need to give an answer to those who sent us. What do you say about yourself?' He said, 'I am the voice of one crying out in the wilderness, 'Make straight the way of the Lord,' as the prophet Isaiah said (Jn 1:19–23).'*

Even though John was certain of his own identity and mission, the Jewish leaders pressed him for answers. When John responded he gave them more than they anticipated,

> *They asked him, 'Then why are you baptizing, if you are neither the Christ, nor Elijah, nor the Prophet?' John answered them, 'I baptize with water, but among you stands one you do not know, even he who comes after me, the strap of whose sandal I am not worthy to untie.' These things took place in Bethany across the Jordan, where John was baptizing. The next day he saw Jesus coming toward him, and said, 'Behold, the Lamb of God, who takes away the sin of the world! This is he of whom I said, 'After me comes a man who ranks before me, because he was before me (Jn 1:25–30).'*

John made it clear who he was and why he had come. He had come to fulfill prophecy and prepare the way for "the Lamb of God, who takes away the sin of the world"—Jesus Christ, the Lord!

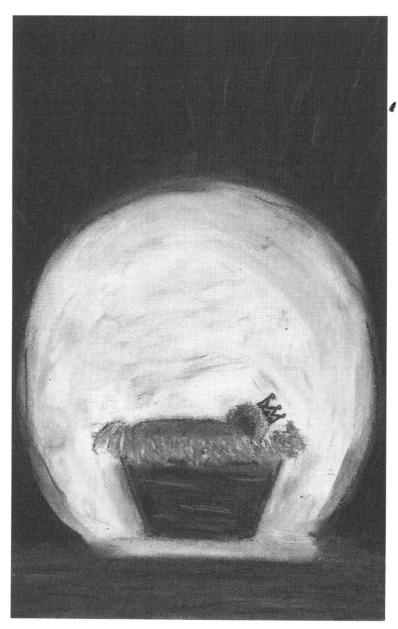

*Heather Boozer • 12ᵗʰ Grade*

# December 10

When I was born, my parents did one of the first things most parents do for their children—they gave me my name: Timothy Paul Dowdy. I have always been grateful for my three names, even when I was called "Timmy" during my childhood years. During my young years I was also called "Little Paul" by some, because I had the temperament of my father.

We have already discussed one of the names of Jesus—"Immanuel," meaning "God with us." Today, let's look at a prophecy in the Old Testament that connects four other names to Jesus. Once again, we turn to the book of Isaiah.

> *In the former time he brought into contempt the land of Zebulun and the land of Naphtali, but in the latter time he has made glorious the way of the sea, the land beyond the Jordan, Galilee of the nations (Is 9:1).*

While this prophecy has a more immediate connection to the history of Israel in the Old Testament, it is also connected to the coming of Jesus in the New Testament.

> *And leaving Nazareth he went and lived in Capernaum by the sea, in the territory of Zebulun and Naphtali, so that what*

> *was spoken by the prophet Isaiah might be fulfilled: 'The land of Zebulun and the land of Naphtali, the way of the sea, beyond the Jordan, Galilee of the Gentiles (Matt 4:13–15).'*

Isaiah contains several prophecies concerning Jesus. For example, in Isaiah 7:14 we learn about the birth of Jesus, and in Isaiah 11, we learn about his kingdom and reign. But the prophecy in Isaiah 9 gives insight into the character of Jesus.

> *For to us a child is born, to us a son is given; and the government shall be upon his shoulder, and his name shall be called Wonderful Counselor, Mighty God, Everlasting Father, Prince of Peace (Is 9:6).*

The first three of these names all speak of the divine nature of Jesus.

"Wonderful Counselor" is an interesting title. "Wonderful" means miraculous or supernatural. As God, Jesus provides counsel that is indeed wonderful. Later in Isaiah we read, "This also comes from the Lord of hosts; he is wonderful in counsel and excellent in wisdom (Is 28:29)."

"Mighty God" is a title that can only describe the Lord God Almighty. Jesus is, without debate, *the* Mighty God.

"Everlasting Father" might sound like a strange thing to call a baby born in Bethlehem, but remember, Jesus is eternal. This phrase actually means "Father of Eternity," which reminds us that Jesus is the sole source of eternal life.

The last name on the list, "Prince of Peace," reminds me of what Jesus said:

*Peace I leave with you; my peace I give to you. Not as the world gives do I give to you. Let not your hearts be troubled, neither let them be afraid (Jn 14:27).*

Jesus is the Wonderful Counselor, Mighty God, Everlasting Father, and Prince of Peace—*with* us and *to* us and *for* us!

No one can give peace the way that Jesus can.

*Jade Holmes • 9th Grade*

# December 17

In 1987, my wife Christie and I were living in Baton Rouge, Louisiana. I was the pastor of a church plant while studying at seminary in New Orleans. Christie was working a full-time job which carried the financial burden for us while I was in school. In the spring of that year we found out that Christie was pregnant with our first, and only, child.

On December 17, 1987, our son—Micah Paul Dowdy—was born weighing in at seven pounds. That night was so exciting! My heart was pounding, my palms were sweating, and I can hardly explain the joy I felt as a new father. But that was only my half the equation. I can still remember the smile on Christie's face when we held Micah up so that she could see him for the very first time. What a beautiful sight!

I am certain Joseph and Mary experienced that same kind of excitement and joy as new parents. Most of the world was completely unaware of the blessing born to them that night in Bethlehem, but there were a few who had the inside story. A host of angels proclaimed the news to a few shepherds out in the fields with their flocks.

*And the angel said to them, "Fear not, for behold, I bring you good news of great joy that will be for all the people. For*

> *unto you is born this day in the city of David a Savior, who is Christ the Lord (Lk 2:10–11).*

Truly, it was the most amazing night the world had ever seen!

Mary and Joseph were devout Jewish parents, so they wanted to obey the law concerning circumcision. That law stated that male children should be circumcised on the eighth day. They obeyed this instruction to honor the Lord. Then, 40 days after Jesus was born, they made their way to the Temple for another ceremony. They were required to participate in a dedication and purification ceremony at the temple in Jerusalem. They made the six-mile journey to Jerusalem to dedicate their son, Jesus, to God. It was at this dedication ceremony they met a man named Simeon.

> *Now there was a man in Jerusalem, whose name was Simeon, and this man was righteous and devout, waiting for the consolation of Israel, and the Holy Spirit was upon him. And it had been revealed to him by the Holy Spirit that he would not see death before he had seen the Lord's Christ. And he came in the Spirit into the temple, and when the parents brought in the child Jesus, to do for him according to the custom of the Law, he took him up in his arms and blessed God and said, 'Lord, now you are letting your servant depart in peace, according to your word; for my eyes have seen your salvation that you have prepared in the presence of all peoples, a light for revelation to the Gentiles, and for glory to your people Israel (Lk 2:25–32).'*

What an amazing meeting! Simeon, a Jew who was considered good, righteous, and devout, said that he had seen the salvation of the Lord when he saw Jesus. He knew what we must all recognize—we are sinners in need of a Savior. When he saw the face of Jesus, he knew that the Savior for all people had come. He had waited and longed to see the promised Messiah. As he held Jesus in his arms, he knew the promise of the Holy Spirit had been fulfilled.

I am reminded again of what the angel told the shepherds the night that Jesus was born:

> *Fear not, for behold, I bring you good news of great joy that will be for all the people. For unto you is born this day in the city of David a Savior, who is Christ the Lord (Lk 2:10–11).*

*Kaylah Bruno • 11ᵗʰ Grade*

# December 18

It's December 18th—only seven days remaining until the best celebration known to mankind. There's something I want you to remember about the unique nature of Christmas as we continue our journey through the scriptures:

*Jesus is Christmas.*

Jesus is the centerpiece of this season, and without him, there is no hope of salvation. But because he came, we can have true hope, salvation, and lasting joy.

In fact, my heart feels joy when I look at the Old Testament prophecies in the about the birth of Jesus. However, one of those prophecies has the opposite emotional effect; it produces great sadness instead of joy. Yet, even through that sadness, we have hope. Why? Because we discover another prophecy about Jesus in the Old Testament.

> *Thus says the Lord:*
> *'A voice is heard in Ramah,*
>     *lamentation and bitter weeping.*
> *Rachel is weeping for her children;*
>     *she refuses to be comforted for her children,*
>     *because they are no more (Jer 31:15).'*

You probably remember the New Testament story about the wise men who came to find the child born King of the Jews. They were following a star in the East, and eventually it led them to the area in Judea where Jesus was born. When they arrived, they met with King Herod to get further clarification about the exact location of this child. Matthew recorded the events this way:

> *Now after Jesus was born in Bethlehem of Judea in the days of Herod the king, behold, wise men from the east came to Jerusalem, saying, 'Where is he who has been born king of the Jews? For we saw his star when it rose and have come to worship him.' When Herod the king heard this, he was troubled, and all Jerusalem with him; and assembling all the chief priests and scribes of the people, he inquired of them where the Christ was to be born. They told him, 'In Bethlehem of Judea, for so it is written by the prophet: 'And you, O Bethlehem, in the land of Judah, are by no means least among the rulers of Judah; for from you shall come a ruler who will shepherd my people Israel.' Then Herod summoned the wise men secretly and ascertained from them what time the star had appeared. And he sent them to Bethlehem, saying, 'Go and search diligently for the child, and when you have found him, bring me word, that I too may come and worship him.' After listening to the king, they went on their way. And behold, the star that they had seen when it rose went before them until it came to rest over the place where the child was. When they saw the star, they rejoiced exceedingly with great joy. And going into the house, they saw the child with Mary his mother, and they fell down and worshiped him. Then, opening their treasures, they offered him gifts, gold and frankincense and myrrh. And being warned in a dream not to return to Herod, they departed to their own country by another way. Now when they had departed, behold, an angel of the Lord appeared to Joseph in a dream and said, 'Rise, take the child*

*and his mother, and flee to Egypt, and remain there until I tell*
*you, for Herod is about to search for the child, to destroy him.'*
*And he rose and took the child and his mother by night and*
*departed to Egypt and remained there until the death of Herod.*
*This was to fulfill what the Lord had spoken by the prophet,*
*'Out of Egypt I called my son. Then Herod, when he saw that*
*he had been tricked by the wise men, became furious, and he sent*
*and killed all the male children in Bethlehem and in all that*
*region who were two years old or under, according to the time*
*that he had ascertained from the wise men. Then was fulfilled*
*what was spoken by the prophet Jeremiah: 'A voice was heard in*
*Ramah, weeping and loud lamentation, Rachel weeping for her*
*children; she refused to be comforted, because they are no more*
*(Matt 2:1–18).'*

Sadly, there is no comfort in the fulfillment of this prophecy. Herod's murderous acts were wicked to the core. And yet, we can still find hope in the truthfulness of the scriptures. Though Herod was not intentionally fulfilling the prophecy recorded by Jeremiah, he did just that.

At the time Jeremiah penned his words of prophecy, they had both an immediate and distant fulfillment. He originally wrote of the great sorrow that would be experienced as the people of Israel were taken by force to Babylon. Ramah was a town about five miles north of Jerusalem. It served as the place where Jewish captives were assembled for deportation to Babylon. "Rachel weeping for her children," was an expression used for all the Jewish mothers who wept over this great defeat. However, according to Matthew, this passage also contained a prophetic message looking forward toward the days when the children of Israel would suffer under the hand of Herod. What occurred in the days of Jeremiah was a type, an illustration, of what occurred during the early days of Jesus' life.

While we find no joy in the evil committed during those days, there is still hope. God provided a way of escape for Jesus and his family by warning Joseph to flee to Egypt. He saved his Son, Jesus, who was born to be the Savior of the world!

*Joseph White • 9<sup>th</sup> Grade*

# December 19

s you can probably see by now, the volume of prophetic evidence relating to the birth of Jesus is amazing. Even more amazing are the number of prophecies that aid us in understanding more about Jesus as God's Son. Many of those prophecies focus on events later in his life.

One of those is the triumphal entry of Jesus into Jerusalem on the Sunday before he was crucified.

> *Rejoice greatly, O daughter of Zion!*
>   *Shout aloud, O daughter of Jerusalem!*
> *Behold, your king is coming to you;*
>   *righteous and having salvation is he,*
> *humble and mounted on a donkey,*
>   *on a colt, the foal of a donkey (Zech 9:9).*

Now, you may read something like that and think it's not very significant . . . but it is. John the Apostle recorded what happened as Jesus came into Jerusalem prior to his crucifixion:

> *The next day the large crowd that had come to the feast heard that Jesus was coming to Jerusalem. So they took branches of palm trees and went out to meet him, crying out, 'Hosanna!*

> *Blessed is he who comes in the name of the Lord, even the King of Israel!' And Jesus found a young donkey and sat on it, just as it is written, 'Fear not, daughter of Zion; behold, your king is coming, sitting on a donkey's colt (Jn 12:12-15)!'*

John used the words, "just as it is written," to help explain the connection between the coming of Jesus into Jerusalem and the prophecy written by Zechariah approximately 500 years before Jesus was born.

The triumphal entry into Jerusalem initiated the final countdown of events in the life of Jesus. However, it is certainly not the way we would expect a king to make his royal entrance. It was on this Palm Sunday that the crowds celebrated Jesus' arrival, believing that he would be the king to deliver them from the oppression of Rome. But that was far from what Jesus came to do.

Matthew described Jesus' humble ride into the city this way:

> *This took place to fulfill what was spoken by the prophet, saying, 'Say to the daughter of Zion, 'Behold, your king is coming to you, humble, and mounted on a donkey, on a colt, the foal of a beast of burden (Mt 21:4–5).'*

Humble. That one word describes the whole of Jesus' life on earth. He humbled himself and was obedient to his Father when he took on flesh and became a man, thereby providing the hope of salvation. The Apostle Paul powerfully underscored the humiliation of Jesus in his letter to the Philippians.

> *Have this mind among yourselves, which is yours in Christ Jesus, who, though he was in the form of God, did not count equality with God a thing to be grasped, but emptied himself,*

*by taking the form of a servant, being born in the likeness of men. And being found in human form, he humbled himself by becoming obedient to the point of death, even death on a cross. Therefore God has highly exalted him and bestowed on him the name that is above every name, so that at the name of Jesus every knee should bow, in heaven and on earth and under the earth, and every tongue confess that Jesus Christ is Lord, to the glory of God the Father (Phil 2:5–11).*

People expect kings to display their power with pomp and circumstance, accompanied by a mighty force and a parade of pride. Jesus displayed real power through his humility. His humble entry into the city not only began the final week of his life; it also revealed the very reason he came. When he came, he humbled himself to the point of death. But this would not be his defeat; it would be the defeat of sin and the grave. Through his death, Jesus satisfied the wrath of God against sin. He paid in full the price of humanity's sin by shedding his own blood on the cross. But, death could not hold him! He rose from the dead to live forever and is now exalted with a "name that is above every name." That name is Jesus, the Savior of the world.

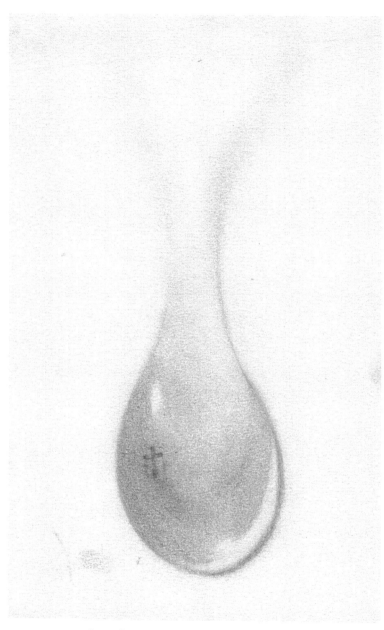

*Jana Caison • Upper School Art Instructor*

# December 20

One advantage we have over the people who lived in Old Testament times is a historical perspective of the events in the life of Jesus. The Jews looked forward to the coming of the Messiah. When the prophets spoke of his coming the Jewish people received the proclamations with great joy. Sadly, when Jesus actually came, the majority of the Jews did not believe he was the Messiah and rejected his message. They longed for the day the Messiah would come, but when he made his appearance their hearts were hard. Their hope had come, but they did not welcome his presence. They refused to believe that Jesus was the one foretold in the prophecies of the past.

The prophets of old wrote and spoke of things that would happen in the future, but most of them did not know the full prophetic implications of their words. That is where we now have the advantage. From where we sit in history, we can read the scriptures and see how the prophecies about Jesus in the Old Testament are fulfilled in the New Testament. The words of God revealed to the Old Testament prophets perfectly described the events of Jesus' birth, life, death, and resurrection as recorded in the New Testament. We now see the full scope of Jesus' incarnation, and when we celebrate his birth at Christmas, our celebration is enriched because we know the rest of the story.

The Treasure of Christmas

Today, I want us to look at a passage in the book of Isaiah that clearly points to Jesus' death on the cross. It is found in Isaiah's detailed description of the Suffering Servant in chapter 53.

> *Who has believed what he has heard from us? And to whom has the arm of the Lord been revealed? For he grew up before him like a young plant, and like a root out of dry ground; he had no form or majesty that we should look at him, and no beauty that we should desire him. He was despised and rejected by men, a man of sorrows and acquainted with grief; and as one from whom men hide their faces he was despised, and we esteemed him not. Surely he has borne our griefs and carried our sorrows; yet we esteemed him stricken, smitten by God, and afflicted. But he was pierced for our transgressions; he was crushed for our iniquities; upon him was the chastisement that brought us peace, and with his wounds we are healed. All we like sheep have gone astray; we have turned—every one—to his own way; and the Lord has laid on him the iniquity of us all (Is 53:1–6).*

As I read those words and reflect on the gospel accounts of Jesus' crucifixion, the reality of the events surrounding the death of Jesus floods my heart. The detail in Isaiah's prophecy is truly supernatural. He wrote those words approximately 600 years before the crucifixion of Jesus, yet he painted an amazingly accurate picture of the circumstances surrounding his death.

The connection between the two passages of scripture reminds us why Jesus came to earth in the first place. The coming of Jesus wasn't a random act without purpose. When Jesus came, it was to fulfill the plan that God revealed to the prophets centuries before it was set in motion. And what was God's purpose?

The words of John the Baptist come to mind, "Behold the lamb of God who takes away the sin of the world (Jn 1:29)." Hallelujah, what a Savior!

*Eunjin Choi • 10ᵗʰ Grade*

# December 21

The birth of Jesus was absolutely amazing! No wonder a star pointed the way for the Magi to worship him. No wonder a host of angels celebrated as they announced the arrival of the King to shepherds watching over their sheep. Throughout the Bible there are pictures of the miraculous birth of Jesus, reminding us again and again that God has always had a plan for salvation. His plan was finally brought into focus when Jesus took on flesh.

Today, let's open the Christmas photo album chronicling the birth of Jesus and take a quick look at a few of my favorite snapshots.

*For God so loved the world, that he gave his only Son, that whoever believes in him should not perish but have eternal life (Jn 3:16).*

This verse sums up the very heartbeat of God the Father toward us. Six simple words—"for God so loved the world." God's motive in sending Jesus always was and is love. It's difficult to grasp the depth of the love God has for us, but we can surely see it displayed in the person of Jesus!

> *But you, O Bethlehem Ephrathah, who are too little to be among the clans of Judah, from you shall come forth for me one who is to be ruler in Israel, whose coming forth is from of old, from ancient days (Micah 5:2).*

> *This passage directs us to the birthplace of Jesus, therefore providing prophetic evidence that Jesus is the Christ! Bethlehem was small but was the perfect place for Jesus to be born.*

> *And behold, you will conceive in your womb and bear a son, and you shall call his name Jesus. He will be great and will be called the Son of the Most High (Lk 1:31-33).*

It had to be quite startling when the angel Gabriel appeared before Mary and announced that she was going to give birth to a child, especially since she was still a virgin. Having a child conceived of the Holy Spirit seemed impossible, except this was the work of God, and nothing is impossible for him! She learned that he would have a kingdom that would never end, and that his name would reveal his purpose. Joseph and Mary would name the child Jesus (Savior) as she had been told by the angel.

> *And the angel said to them, "Fear not, for behold, I bring you good news of great joy that will be for all the people (Lk 2:10)."*

When the angel spoke to the shepherds that night I'm certain he had their complete attention. The shepherds' faces revealed the same emotion we all would have felt—fear. But the angel told them there was nothing to fear. The message the angel had come to deliver was "good news." What a powerful reminder that whenever we tell people about Jesus, it is good news!

*When they saw the star, they rejoiced exceedingly with great joy. And going into the house they saw the child with Mary his mother, and they fell down and worshiped him. Then, opening their treasures, they offered him gifts, gold and frankincense and myrrh (Mt 2:10-11).*

"When they saw the star" the wise men knew something amazing had happened, which reminds us that the birth of Jesus was the supernatural work of Almighty God.

*But when the fullness of time had come, God sent forth his Son, born of woman, born under the law, to redeem those who were under the law, so that we might receive adoption as sons (Gal 4:4-5).*

This power packed passage, written by the Apostle Paul, reveals several truths about our Savior:

- Jesus came with purpose—*"God sent."*
- Jesus is fully divine—*"God sent forth his Son."*
- Jesus is fully man—*"born of woman."*
- Jesus is perfectly righteous in every way—*"born under the law."*
- Jesus came to redeem us—*"to redeem."*
- We are redeemed to become members of God's family—*"so that we might receive adoption as sons."*

When we view them together as a perfectly arranged collection, these pictures of Christ joyously proclaim that the birth of Jesus changed everything on the night when hope was born.

*Weronika Hipp • 9ᵗʰ Grade*

# December 22

I spent most of my childhood growing up in the same house; it was located in the suburbs just north of downtown Tallahassee, Florida. My two sisters and I had the privilege of being raised in a home where both of our parents were Christians. My mother stayed at home to raise the three of us. My father worked as an auditor for the state of Florida. He worked Monday through Friday, 8:00 AM to 5:00 PM, just like clockwork. I can't say for sure, since I was just a kid, but I think the same pressures that impact parents today weighed on my parents as well.

In spite of the demands of their daily responsibilities, they led our home with a commitment to make sure we understood the Gospel. We were deeply involved in our church family. Although there were times during my teenage years when I pushed back against my parents' insistence that we go to church, I never won by protest. Now, I'm so thankful that they never relented. It was through their consistent witness, the ministry of the church, and the work of the Holy Spirit that I came to know Christ as my Savior. I will be forever grateful to them for sharing Jesus with me and my sisters through their words and their walk. To be a child in the home of Paul and Lonease Dowdy was a blessing indeed.

I could fill the pages of this book with the things my parents did to shape my life through their godly impact. Today, I just want to tell you about one. Our home was pretty normal. By that I mean we were not perfect people or the perfect family. In other words, we had our ups and downs. There were days when the relationships at home were peaceful and pleasant . . . and then there were the other days. You know what I mean? Days when trouble ruled the roost. However, even on the roller coaster of life as a family, there was one thing I always knew—my dad and mom loved me. How? They told me. My mom told me as only a mother can when she talks to her son. My dad told me. Even though I was taller than him by the eighth grade, he always made sure I knew that he loved me—even in the tough times. Because of their influence, I have made that practice a consistent part of my own life. I try to tell my wife, my son, my daughter-in-law, and my grandsons in every conversation that I love them. And you know what? I have never regretted saying, "I love you."

Not only did my parents verbally express their love for me, they also backed up their words with actions. Even when we didn't see eye to eye, I knew that my parents still loved me. There were times when their actions were filled with discipline, and other times when they were filled with mercy. Still, I always knew that they loved me.

As I think about both my childhood and my adulthood, the one thing I treasure most is that I have never gone to bed without the calm assurance that my parents loved me. What a priceless gift!

Then I think about the birth of Jesus, and I reflect on what God communicated to me when he sent his one and only son. In that priceless act of sacrifice, our Heavenly Father simply said, "I love you."

That reminds me of something the Apostle John wrote late in his life,

*In this the love of God was made manifest among us, that God sent his only Son into the world, so that we might live through him (1 Jn 4:9).*

And it reminds me of what Paul wrote about God's love in the book of Romans,

*For I am sure that neither death nor life, nor angels nor rulers, nor things present nor things to come, nor powers, nor height nor depth, nor anything else in all creation, will be able to separate us from the love of God in Christ Jesus our Lord (Rom 8:38–39).*

In sending Jesus, God said to the world, "I love you." As children of God we can be assured that nothing in this life or the life to come will separate us from the amazing love of God!

*Savannah Fallaw • 9ᵗʰ Grade*

# December 23

When we think about the passages in Bible detailing the events of the birth of Jesus, Matthew 1 and Luke 2 are usually the first that come to mind. These two passages lay out the dramatic events surrounding the birth of Jesus. But there is another section of scripture found in the Gospels that describes of the birth of Jesus in another way. It isn't a narrative passage describing the night Jesus was born; rather, it is an announcement of Jesus' incarnation, which helps us understand the purpose and power of his arrival. This passage is found in the opening chapter of the Gospel of John:

> *In the beginning was the Word, and the Word was with God, and the Word was God. He was in the beginning with God. All things were made through him, and without him was not any thing made that was made. In him was life, and the life was the light of men. . . . And the Word became flesh and dwelt among us, and we have seen his glory, glory as of the only Son from the Father, full of grace and truth. (John bore witness about him, and cried out, 'This was he of whom I said, 'He who comes after me ranks before me, because he was before me.') For from his fullness we have all received, grace upon grace. For the law was given through Moses; grace and truth*

*came through Jesus Christ. No one has ever seen God; the only God, who is at the Father's side, he has made him known (Jn 1:1-4, 14-18).*

It is hard to imagine what life was like for the Apostle John. He experienced much in his life, but it's clear from these words that the most remarkable thing he ever witnessed was the life and ministry of Jesus. John described it as the "glory" of Jesus, and he stressed that he was there to see it all! At first glance, it appears that verse 15 is an odd interruption. However, John purposefully inserted this reference to John the Baptist to add another eye witness to the "glory" of Jesus' life on earth. In fact, John the Apostle used John the Baptist's own words to remind us of something he said in the very first verse—the coming of Jesus in the flesh is so glorious because of his eternal existence with God.

The words John used paint a powerful picture. Jesus "became flesh." This reminds us that the eternal, divine Word became fully human, born as a baby in Bethlehem. Jesus, fully human, was the embodiment of the name "Immanuel" which means "God with us."

To say that Jesus' coming to earth as a man is unique grossly understates the point John expressed. Jesus was one of a kind for all time. His coming wasn't simply remarkable; it was a miracle. John stressed that point in verse 16 when he wrote that we have all been blessed by his coming. How? Jesus came with the full measure of "grace and truth." There was grace in the law but not the full measure of grace Jesus showed us. Jesus was the embodiment of God's loving-kindness, as well as his other attributes. Jesus revealed how God helps us through grace and truth. Jesus met all the requirements of the law because he was God in the flesh. And, in his grace and truth, he displayed his love to those who could never deserve it—that is undeserved favor.

As John wrapped up the prologue to his Gospel, he used verse 18 to make the most powerful statement about the coming of Jesus. Without Jesus, there is no other way that we could have known God. Jesus is the one who made him known. John tells us that no one, not even Moses, has seen God. But Jesus made him known.

The writer of Hebrews put it this way:

*Long ago, at many times and in many ways, God spoke to our fathers by the prophets, but in these last days he has spoken to us by his Son, whom he appointed the heir of all things, through whom also he created the world. He is the radiance of the glory of God and the exact imprint of his nature, and he upholds the universe by the word of his power. After making purification for sins, he sat down at the right hand of the Majesty on high (Heb 1:1–3).*

Jesus is the glorious and true treasure of Christmas!

*Mallory Poorman • 10<sup>th</sup> Grade*

# December 24

For years now, our family tradition on Christmas Eve has started with a trip to church. We gather with our church family, sing Christmas carols, share the Lord's Supper, and read the Christmas story from Luke 2. We end the night by singing the well-known hymn, "Silent Night," while we light candles, bringing bright light to an otherwise dark room. It is one of my favorite worship services of the year. After that, we all head to my dad's house to enjoy the evening together. We open a few gifts with the grandkids, have great conversations, and share the rest of the night around the dinner table.

Over time you've probably developed some Christmas traditions as well, or perhaps your Christmas Eve looks different from year to year. Whether you have long-standing traditions or not, I want to invite you to start a great tradition today—wherever you are, whoever you're with, read the story of Jesus' birth together from the Bible on Christmas Eve. It isn't long but it sure is amazing. You can find it on the opening page of the New Testament in the book of Matthew.

*Now the birth of Jesus Christ took place in this way. When his mother Mary had been betrothed to Joseph, before they came together she was found to be with child from the Holy Spirit.*

*And her husband Joseph, being a just man and unwilling to put her to shame, resolved to divorce her quietly. But as he considered these things, behold, an angel of the Lord appeared to him in a dream, saying, "Joseph, son of David, do not fear to take Mary as your wife, for that which is conceived in her is from the Holy Spirit. She will bear a son, and you shall call his name Jesus, for he will save his people from their sins." All this took place to fulfill what the Lord had spoken by the prophet: "Behold, the virgin shall conceive and bear a son, and they shall call his name Immanuel" (which means, God with us). When Joseph woke from sleep, he did as the angel of the Lord commanded him: he took his wife, but knew her not until she had given birth to a son. And he called his name Jesus (Matt 1:18-25).*

I love how this section of scripture ends: "And they called his name Jesus." Jesus was very common name in New Testament times, and it had deep roots in Jewish culture. His name meant "Yahweh saves." The Bible makes it clear that Jesus is the source of salvation for everyone who believes in him. There are several places in the New Testament that reveal this.

*But these are written so that you may believe that Jesus is the Christ, the Son of God, and that by believing you may have life in his name (Jn 20:31).*

*And there is salvation in no one else, for there is no other name under heaven given among men by which we must be saved (Acts 4:12).*

*And this is the testimony, that God gave us eternal life, and this life is in his Son. Whoever has the Son has life; who-*

*ever does not have the Son of God does not have life (1 Jn 5:11–12).*

Jesus is more than a good man, a moral example, a gifted teacher, a wise philosopher, or an excellent leader. He is God in human form—the Savior of sinners and hope of the world.

On this Christmas Eve, I hope you remember the birth of our Savior and look forward to a great Christmas Day celebration with your family and friends tomorrow!

*Emily Stuber • 11ᵗʰ Grade*

# December 25

Merry Christmas! I hope you and your family enjoy a wonderful day celebrating the birth of Jesus. As I think back on my childhood and our family Christmas celebrations, one stands out. We lived in Florida, so the weather on Christmas Day certainly wasn't "spiteful," as the old song goes. I instead, it was a pretty average winter day in North Florida—80 degrees with lots of sunshine. Our house had one main hallway that connected the living room with all the bedrooms. It was there that my sisters and I waited each year for permission to rush into the living room and unwrap our presents. That short run down the hallway was always filled with anticipation and excitement.

It was still dark outside on that Christmas morning when our parents said "Go!" When I turned the corner, I could see the silhouette of something leaning by the tree. It was a bicycle—the very thing I'd been hoping to receive! In my mind, it was the best Christmas ever. I almost forgot to look at anything else, I was so mesmerized by my shiny, green bike. And the best part was that the weather outside was nice enough to ride my new bike on Christmas Day—what could be better than that?

Sadly, just a few days later, my bike was stolen from our front porch, and I learned one of life's great lessons—our greatest earthly treasures don't last forever.

Does anything last forever? Yes, but only one thing—the salvation that comes through Jesus. So, on this day we celebrate the greatest gift of all. Let's read the record of Jesus birth as recorded by Dr. Luke:

*In those days a decree went out from Caesar Augustus that all the world should be registered. This was the first registration when Quirinius was governor of Syria. And all went to be registered, each to his own town. And Joseph also went up from Galilee, from the town of Nazareth, to Judea, to the city of David, which is called Bethlehem, because he was of the house and lineage of David, to be registered with Mary, his betrothed, who was with child. And while they were there, the time came for her to give birth. And she gave birth to her firstborn son and wrapped him in swaddling cloths and laid him in a manger, because there was no place for them in the inn. And in the same region there were shepherds out in the field, keeping watch over their flock by night. And an angel of the Lord appeared to them, and the glory of the Lord shone around them, and they were filled with great fear. And the angel said to them, "Fear not, for behold, I bring you good news of great joy that will be for all the people. For unto you is born this day in the city of David a Savior, who is Christ the Lord. And this will be a sign for you: you will find a baby wrapped in swaddling cloths and lying in a manger." And suddenly there was with the angel a multitude of the heavenly host praising God and saying, "Glory to God in the highest, and on earth peace among those with whom he is pleased!" When the angels went away from them into heaven, the shepherds said to one another, "Let us go over to Bethlehem and see this thing that has happened, which the Lord has made known to us." And they went with haste and found Mary and Joseph, and the baby lying in a manger. And when they saw it, they made known the saying that had been told them concerning this child. And all who heard it wondered at what the shepherds told them. But Mary treasured up all these things, pondering them in her heart. And the shepherds returned, glorifying and praising God for all they had heard and seen, as it had been told them (Lk 2:1-20).*

Christmas is the day to glorify and praise God for all that we've experienced through the person of Jesus. He is, as the saying goes, "The reason for the season." Christmas is the most wonderful time of the year, because Jesus is the true treasure of Christmas.

Merry Christmas! I pray that today you enjoy celebrating the birth of Jesus, our Savior, our King.

# Finding L.I.F.E. in Jesus!

*E*veryone wants to be happy. The hard part is determining exactly what that means. For some, happiness is defined through relationships. They believe that popularity, a huge friend list on Facebook, and a significant other produces happiness. For others, happiness is defined through success. They believe that personal achievement, a huge number in their bank account, and plenty of expensive toys produces happiness. For still others, happiness is defined through community. They believe that personal growth, a huge impact for societal change, and embracing diversity produces happiness. And these things do—until they don't.

Experiencing happiness is as difficult as catching the greased pig at the county fair. It appears to be right in front of us, but then it slips through our fingers and is gone. Friends, achievement, and personal growth have the potential to bring happiness into our lives, but when our friends disappear, success eludes us, and we realize that we're incapable of self-transformation, happiness is quickly replaced by disillusionment and depression. The problem with pursuing happiness is that it is an emotion that is driven by our circumstances. And let's be honest—we all tend to have more negative than positive experiences in our lives.

So, what's the answer? Should we keep doing the same things while expecting different results, or should we consider what Jesus has to say about finding our purpose for life? If you want to stay on the hamster wheel while you try to catch up to happiness, you can stop reading here. But if you're ready to consider what God wants to do in your life, please read on.

God never promises happiness in the Bible. Are you surprised to hear that? Instead, he promises something much greater—joy. While happiness is an emotion fueled by circumstance, joy is an attitude fueled by God's Spirit. Happiness is self-determined. In other words, I am the sole determiner of whether I'm happy at any given moment. Joy, on the other hand, is God-determined. God has promised to give us joy, and it isn't based on our circumstances—it's based on God's character and promises.

This is why Jesus never talks about giving people happiness. He knew all too well that chasing happiness is like chasing your shadow. You can never catch it. Instead, he talks about giving people life. He said, "I came that they may have life and have it abundantly (Jn 10:10)." Here, Jesus reveals that the thing people really want, whether they know it or not, is abundant life. To have an abundant life means that you are personally satisfied in all areas of your life, and you experience peace and contentment as a result. Jesus' statement also means that we do not have the capacity to create that kind of life for ourselves. Jesus came in order to give it to us. But how? The Bible tells us that achieving this kind of satisfied life requires us to know something about God, ourselves, and the reason for the death and resurrection of Jesus Christ.

First, we must understand God's **love**. The Bible says that God is love (I Jn 4:8), and God created us so that we could know him and experience his love (Gen 1:26-31). God created us to be worshipers and to live forever in the reality of his glory. And, when sin marred his perfect creation, he created a plan to free men and women from its curse. At just the right time in history, God sent his own Son, Jesus, into our world. "For God so loved the world, that he gave his only Son, that whoever believes in him should not perish but have eternal life (Jn 3:16)." It is God's love that motivates him to restore relationship with those who are separated from him by sin.

Second, we must understand our **isolation**. To be isolated is to be separated from someone, and as a result, to be alone. This is what sin has done to us. It has separated us from the very one we were created to know, love, and worship—God. When Adam and Eve rebelled against God by breaking the lone command he had given them, the entire world was brought under the curse of sin (Gen 3). As a result, God removed them from the Garden of Eden, and their perfect fellowship with God was broken. In an instant, they had become isolated from God because of their sin. From that moment to this, every person born into this world is guilty of sin. The Bible says, "For all have sinned and fall short of the glory of God (Rom 3:23)." Because of this "there is none righteous, no, not one (Rom 3:10)." Further, "The wages of sin is death (Rom 6:23a)." We were created to love and worship God in perfect community, but now because of sin we are isolated from him. Meanwhile, we try to satisfy this desire to know God by pursuing our own happiness, even though we can never hope to attain it. And in doing so, we risk being isolated from God for all eternity.

Third, we must understand our need for **forgiveness.** There is only one way to experience God's love and escape the isolation caused by sin—we must experience God's forgiveness. In spite of sin, God never stopped loving the people he created. He promised Adam and Eve that he would send someone who could fix the problem they had created. When it was time, God sent his own Son, Jesus, to be the world's Savior. This, too, was an act of God's love. The Bible says, "God shows his love for us in that while we were still sinners, Christ died for us (Rom 5:8)." When Jesus died on the cross, he was paying the penalty for our sins (Rom 3:23-26). When God raised Jesus from the dead, it was to demonstrate that forgiveness was available to all who would receive it by faith. Paul explains how this happens in his letter to the Ephesians. "For by grace you have been saved through faith. And this is not your own doing; it is the gift of God, not a result of works, so that no one may boast (Eph 2:8-9)."

The reality is that we cannot experience salvation as a result of our own efforts. We can try to be a good person, go to a church, even give a ton of money to worthy causes—none of these "works" can provide forgiveness. No matter how hard we try, we will always "fall short of the glory of God." That is why we must receive God's offer of forgiveness and salvation by faith. Faith simply means to trust or believe. Salvation requires us to believe that God loves us, that we are isolated from him by our sins, and that his Son Jesus died and was raised to life again to pay the sin debt that we owe God because of our sins. When we take God up on his offer of the gift of salvation, he doesn't just give us forgiveness—he gives us life! The Bible says, "The free gift of God is eternal life in Christ Jesus our Lord (Rom 6:23)."

Fourth, we must understand the **enjoyment** that comes from knowing, loving, and worshiping God. Whether we know it or not, we are slaves to sin until God sets us free (Rom 6:20-23). This was the ultimate reason that God sent his Son, Jesus, to die on the cross for our sins—God sent Jesus so that we could be set free from our sins. Jesus said, "You will know the truth, and the truth will set you free. . . . Everyone who commits sin is a slave to sin. . . . So, if the Son sets you free, you will be free indeed (Jn 8:32-36)." Jesus was teaching us that we must be set free from sin in order to enjoy the life that God has given us—both now and in eternity future. We are set free when we commit our lives to Jesus

Christ through faith in his death and resurrection. Then, and only then, will we find joy in the abundant life of Jesus Christ!

So, the question for you is a simple one: Are you ready to experience freedom from sin and the abundant life that Jesus promised you? If so, God is waiting for to talk with him about it (Jer 29:13). Stop right where you are and make this your prayer to God,

> "Father in heaven, I know that I'm a sinner. I know that I've done lots of things that displease you and disappoint you. And, I know that I'm isolated from you because of my sin. I know that if I die without knowing you, I will spend forever separated from you in hell. But, I believe that Jesus is your sinless Son, and I believe that he died on the cross for me. I believe that he died to provide a perfect payment for my sin debt. I believe that you raised him from the dead so that I could experience forgiveness for my sins. Right now, Father, I'm asking you to forgive me of my sins and save me. I am receiving your Son Jesus as my personal Lord and Savior. I will follow you the rest of my life. Please give me the joy of a life spent knowing, loving, and worshiping you. I ask these things in Jesus' name, Amen."

If you made the decision to accept Jesus as your Savior today, we want to talk with you! Please contact the people at www. seed-publishing-group.com. We would love to talk with you about your decision and help you with your first steps in following Jesus!

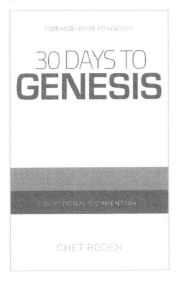

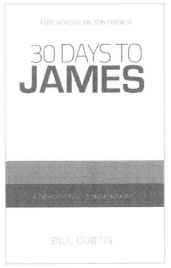

*Also from 30 Days to the Bible:*

*30 Days to Deuteronomy*
*by Matt Rogers*

• • •

*30 Days to Jeremiah*
*by Gary Yates*

• • •

*30 Days to Acts*
*by Doug Munton*

81069705R00074

Made in the USA
Columbia, SC
24 November 2017